Copyright © 2025 by MC Augstkalns

All rights reserved.

No portion of this book may be reproduced in any form without written permission from the author, except as permitted by U.S. copyright law.

No portion of this book may be used to train artificial intelligence or machine learning systems, now or in the future. Permission for such use will not be granted under any circumstances, during the copyright term and thereafter.

Book Cover by GetCovers.com

Illustrations and images by MC Augstkalns.

First edition 2025

To my parents, for providing much of the
material for this book, hopefully unintentionally.

And to Tanya, who was there to pick up the pieces.

This is Not Ideal
A Year of Coping Skills

By MC Augstkalns

Table of Contents

Water

I'm squeezing out all of the water
The tears and the blood
The deluge and flood
The rain from the years
And all of the tears
That I've shed
The fears
The pain
The shame
The guilt
All of the hatred and none of the good
Self-loathing and doubt
I'll have it all figured out
I was floating on paper
My children will ride upon boats

3-24-24

I Am Sorry…

for being too loud

for being too much

for being in the way

for taking up too much space

for bothering anybody

for making so much noise

for all of the chaos I bring

for the inconvenience

for my demeanor

for my tone

for the way I am perceived

for the way I perceive the world

for my inability to accept your love

for my lack of whatever it was you needed

I am sorry
for being…

3-24-24

You

Astronomers say that when solar systems form, the violence of this great celestial birthing can sometimes send a new planet careening off in the vast depths of interstellar space, alone and frozen into the void, to be lost forever. Before we met, *that* was me…

The moment we first kissed, a fiery sun erupted at the center of my universe, and suddenly, I was no longer lost and alone. Suddenly, I had an orbit, a purpose; I wheeled around you and you alone.

When our eyes met, yours contained galaxies—multitudes. Infinite universes I could lose myself in ceaselessly. I lost my breath, but I found I did not die. In fact, I lived.

Though stars may burn out and the universe may end, love is eternal. You have promised me an eternity. And still, that is only your second greatest gift to me. Thank you for you—just *you*.

3-25-24

Mother

Mister Rogers once said,
"Love is an action noun, like struggle."
It's something we choose
like work or play.
Sometimes, I wonder how I got to be 36 years old
and never stopped choosing you
And while our lives overlapped,
You
Never
Chose
Me.

3-27-24

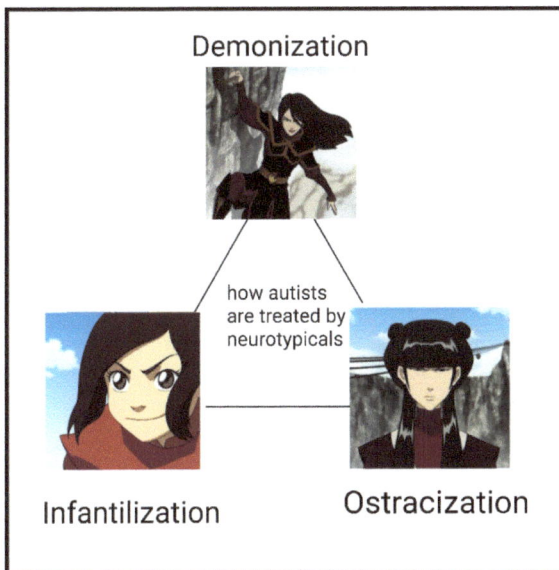

"Calm Down"

Don't think,
Don't feel,
Don't touch,
Don't be.

Be seen, not heard.
Be perfect, not good.

Emotionless,
Calm,
Steady.

Inside,
I am too much—
Too great,
Too loud.

So be quiet.
Don't shout.
Don't talk.
Be as quiet as a mouse.

Be quieter!

Be invisible.
Don't exist.
Be the negative space between thoughts,
Between words,
Between feelings.

I am a scaffolding.
I am here to support you—
Only you,
Never me.

3-30-24

Dear Tanuishka,

You are calm
Peace
A loving embrace
Warmth
Joy—
All that is well with my soul

In your eyes, I find strength
When I cannot find it within
Your grace extends to me
When I cannot find it inside myself
Your exquisite beauty reminds me to seek my own
And the breathtaking beauty of the world
You give me hope, passion,
Steadiness, and will

You are the song in my spirit
My light, my life
My reason for pressing onwards
I breathe because of you
Forever and always—

Love,
    MCishka

3-31-24

Profession

"What do you do?"
I'm an
       Artist,
       Linguist,
       Writer,
       Poet,
       Teacher,
       Influencer,
       Volunteer,
       Researcher,
       Gamer…

More precisely,
I've spent 36 years
Actively trying
Not
To fall
Apart.

4-1-24

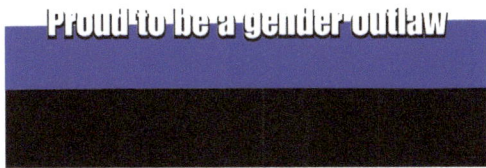

Proud to be a gender outlaw

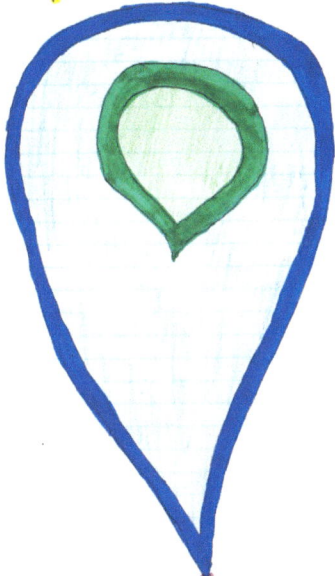

Define "Happiness"

It is choosing a movie from the endless rows of bootleg video tapes and DVDs Mr. Kafka made from the library and Blockbuster and Netflix, on shelves in the musty basement, sitting on the futon with him and Kathleen and Walter with homemade coffee ice cream and getting lost in another world. *But then the plane crashed and—*

It is jumping off the high-dive every summer, sinking to the bottom of the deep end, 13 feet deep, breath-holding contests with Kathleen, waving back and forth or guessing what word the other was shouting underwater. *But dead girls don't shout…*

It is, unexpectedly, a GameCube on Christmas morning the year I'm fourteen, the year I thought, maybe just maybe joy was returning after Mommy died. Santa was coming back, and I wouldn't have to hold up holidays alone anymore. *But I never saw Santa again…*

It is walking down the street in Oslo one night in mid-June, drunk and confused by the lack of nighttime and very unfluent in Norwegian, and being so surprised to find a street busker singing *Country Roads*, the only English I've heard thus far, that I shove an entire wad of meaningless kroner into his guitar case as I sing along. *But then the sun is reappearing, far too soon, and it's time for bed anyway, so off I go…*

"Does it ever last?" you ask.
"Does anything?" I reply.

4-4-24

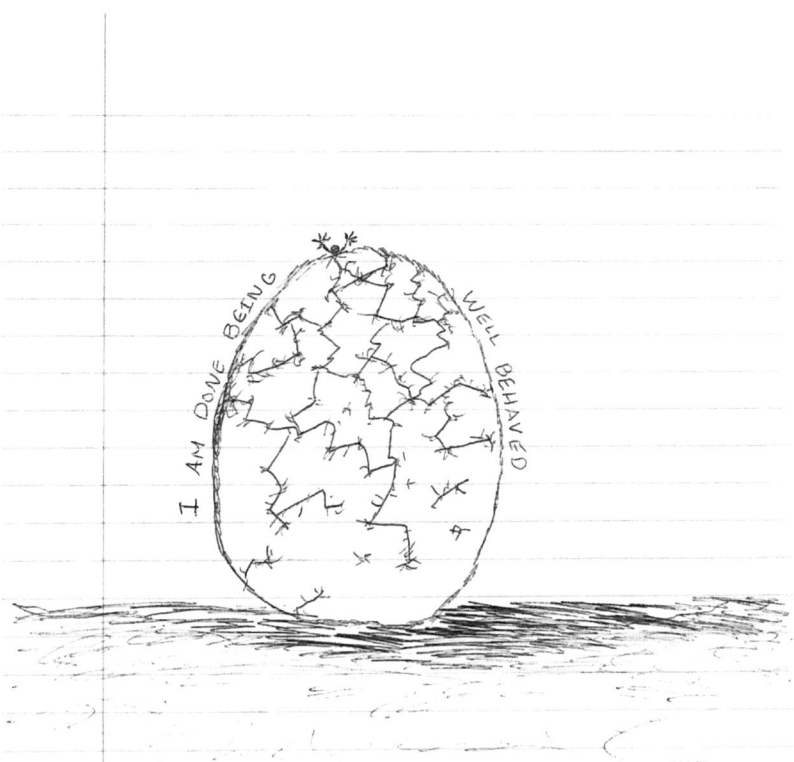

To My Reader

In case nobody mentioned it today
Or ever:
You deserve love.
You deserve life.
You are worthy,
Irreplaceable,
A miracle.

The universe chose *you*
As a means of pondering itself
Out of infinite possibilities—
Isn't that unique?

In all of fathomless time,
You are here
Now.
You will never *be* again.
Don't throw that away,
no matter how much you may want to.
Our lives are overlapping, yours and mine,
And that is a miracle too.

4-4-24

This Mask Is Growing Heavy, Reader

In the beginning, God created the Heavens and the Earth. That was one of the first things I learned. Later, I heard other stories about vast turtles, myriad pantheons, explosions lost so far in the depths of time that they are nigh unreachable. The one thing I gleaned from all of them was that perfection devolved instantly to chaos.

That made sense because my life was a fragile feather adrift in a storm-tossed sea, trapped on the surface most of the time and occasionally being pulled under only to resurface. Sometimes, it would emerge into the eye of the hurricane, which was constantly moving, changing, shifting about. I called this hurricane, "Mommy." The calm was unpredictable, the violence of the storm less foreign to me. Have you ever tried to hug a thunderhead?

My father... was God in the way I understood God to be: a man in the sky who you begged to intervene, but he was too busy doing other things to take notice, unless perhaps to judge you if you were to die before you wake. I knew I was lacking, because if I wasn't, God would notice me, wouldn't He? God spoke to the people around me; they said so all the time. I never heard Him. Daddy was too busy; God was too busy... There was a pervasive loneliness.

Longing.

An angel, a spoiled brat... so many labels. Nobody could pin me down. I was in second, third grade and already so guarded, so masked, the walls so high nothing in China could compare. Friends? How? I must keep up appearances...

So alone.

So full of fury, now, at the blindness of my community.

A child, an autistic child in particular... they don't lie. They may be so perfectly trained in *etiquette* and *protocol* and outward perception, but they are still a child, and children, they say things.

If I said something, and you heard it...
If you saw something, and you didn't act...
You are responsible.

I couldn't hide the years of dissociation after the Hurricane finally left my life for good. I couldn't hide my tears, flinching at raised hands and voices, being so lost in my own world that I couldn't connect with this one.

Where were you?

I just.
I can't.

Jnhmm hc hmm B ffssidskkfasukdbvjvv

fart noises and raspberries and incoherent spluttering

…

My apologies, dear Reader.

I'm good now.

Hey, did you know I'm a linguist?

They say I have a way with words.

4-5-24

You know, for a religion with a central story about an object or idea being forbidden, and humanity's response to that, I feel like y'all failed to understand the assignment

"No s3x before marriage"

"Never take the Lord's name in vain"

"Absolutely no alcohol/dr*gs/caffeine/etc"

"Meat on Fridays is forbidden"

Last Name

My last name is Augstkalns.

Or possibly…

Augustkalns
Augstains
Austkalins
Augustkain

No, wait, it's…

Agustkalns
Augustkins
Augstkalts
Augstklins

Aha! I've got it!

Oxcond.

4-5-24

Flashback

I'm sitting on my bed
Writing,
Thinking.

Suddenly

I am 22 months old and 36 years old at the same time,
Rediscovering something for the first time in a lifetime.

Who knew those old Spot books could put up a fight?

I resurface,
gasping for breath.

My chest feels as though
a giant chunk has been cleaved from it—
Physically carved out, raw
An open, gaping wound

Yet

Clean.

The breaths are coming more easily than they ever have.

I don't feel weaker this time.
This time, remembering,
re-experiencing has brought strength
This is just a taste.

I smile to myself as I think,
"I can go deeper."

4-5-24

Eclipse

Today
I danced and whooped and hollered in a field in Ohio
As the Sun disappeared for three minutes in the middle of the day—
A truly primitive and primeval response to such a happening,
But my brain offered up no other response,
And frankly, it shouldn't have been expected to
Given the general permanence of the Sun.

I'd seen the Sun go out once before
And thought I'd know what to expect.
Figured I'd be more dignified this time,
Greet the midday night with more decorum.

Nope!

Afterwards, when the Sun re-emerged,
the people greeted it with first cheers
And clapping for about a minute,
Then immediately headed to the exit.
The show was over;
Nothing to see here…

Having viewed the Sun's party trick
next to a museum, I went inside,
Where I

Had a panic attack.

So many people

All around

Walking every which way.

This was not a predictable motion
like the dance of the Heavens, and so I fell apart
(Autism and PTSD being a bitch like that)
My friend drove me home, through her own troubles,
and now I sit deposited on my own bed.

And as I think back,

The memory of Apollo's wrath,
of the great dragon swallowing the Sun
Is already beginning to fade—
Though it was fewer than eight hours ago.

And I wonder if there are some things
Humanity was not meant to hold in our minds…
And if that is the true meaning of "eclipse"…

4-8-24

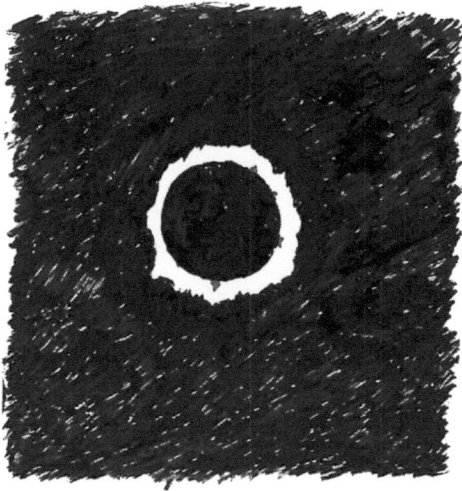

neglected

i'm
mentally:

emotionally
motionless,
petrified,
tormented...
yoked

4-10-24

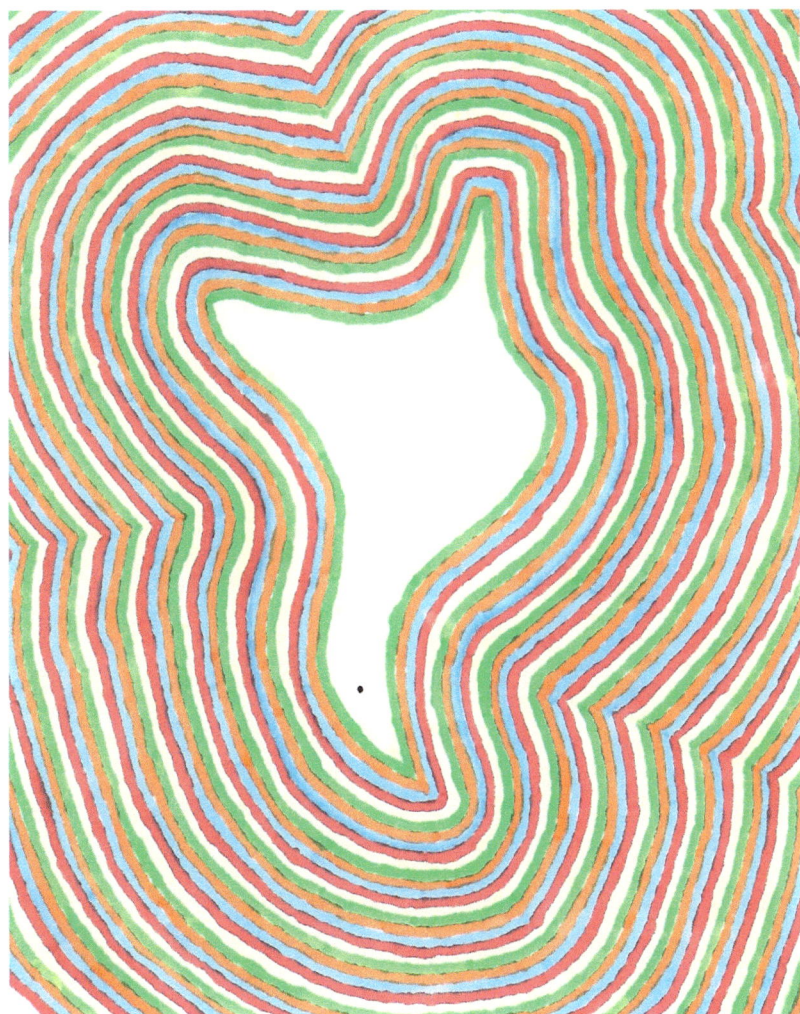

Public Services

When I was little,
The only time I ever heard "thank you" was while watching PBS.
My favorite shows were only possible thanks to Viewers Like Me.
Even at three and four,
I knew that there was something off about this praise
And yet, I basked in it
Because something in me ached
When the nice man said it.

———

The first time I heard I was valuable
Was when I was five years old.
It was fire safety week in kindergarten.
A fireman came with a portable house.
He warned us things might get scary,
Taught us what to do if our houses caught fire and then
Filled the little house with bubblegum-scented smoke
And helped us escape.
The other children were frightened
Only placated with the coloring book and toy hat.
But me?
I had gleaned something before:
"If your house catches fire, what do you take?" he'd asked
And some children had guessed toys or books or clothes
Until the nice fireman had said the answer was *nothing*
Because our parents could get new Things,
But they could never get new Us's.
We were one of a kind and irreplaceable.
I had genuinely never considered this before and
Armed with the thought that I meant anything,
The coloring book and hat were mere tokens.

———

I began to read when I was quite young,
Less than three years old—
Haltingly
And then all at once, devouring anything with words printed on it.
Libraries became my refuge;
I am still convinced librarians are superheroes.

Greek mythology? ESP? Astronomy?
Dinosaurs? Geology?
(Very specifically) the Saguaro cactus?
I devoured as much as I could even before first grade.
The children's section? Bah!
The library was freedom.
It was another world.
There were no shackles there.
The only limits were my mind
And how many books there were,
And I was pretty sure both were infinite.

———

Looking back, the people who were there for me
Had no idea that they ever served a purpose,
And the people who thought they were there
Served little to none.
I don't know if it's that way for everyone,
But I do know
That they say it takes a village to raise a child
And certainly,
If you refuse to do it yourself,
The child will be raised anyway,
So be sure to train your villagers well.

4-18-24

Transactional Economy

Gas costs how much? In this economy?
Do you realize there's not even a dollar menu anymore?
Have you seen the cost of groceries?
I'm expected to pay how much for rent?
And my salary is what now?
How is any of this reasonable?
Healthcare is too expensive,
Taxes are too high,
They get us coming and going,
Streaming is turning into cable again,
Corporations are out for our last cent...
The horrors of late-stage capitalism.
They are killing us all.

I nod in agreement,
Because you aren't wrong,
Then sign the check.
Send the CashApp, the Venmo, the PayPal.
Buy the dinner, the gas, the groceries, the gift
So that you will continue to be
My friend.

4-19-24

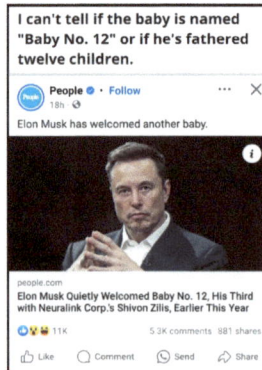

I can't tell if the baby is named "Baby No. 12" or if he's fathered twelve children.

People ● · Follow
18h · 🌐
Elon Musk has welcomed another baby.

people.com
Elon Musk Quietly Welcomed Baby No. 12, His Third with Neuralink Corp.'s Shivon Zilis, Earlier This Year

11K   5.3K comments   881 shares

👍 Like   💬 Comment   📞 Send   ↪ Share

The Definition of Insanity

I don't know why
I open up to people,
Act vulnerable,
Bare myself
Over and over again
Expecting a different outcome
When it never stops blowing up in my face…

But I guess that's why I keep ending up in psych wards, huh?

4-29-24

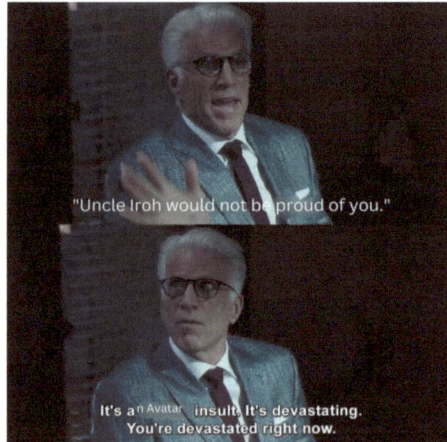

"Uncle Iroh would not be proud of you."

It's an Avatar insult. It's devastating. You're devastated right now.

Karma

"What goes around, comes around."
Isn't that what you taught me, Mommy?
I thought at the time it meant
Be nice to people
And treat them well,
Believing my kindness would return to me someday.

As I grew up, I learned other words for this:
Karma,
The Golden Rule,
"Do unto others as you would have them do unto you."
It existed in every religion I researched,
Came out of every adult's mouth.

Be kind,
Be good,
Be wise,
Be fair,
Be righteous,
Be just.

Now, here's the thing:
I'm autistic, not clueless.
I'm great at following directions.
But the rest of you? *Not so much.*
If vaccines actually did cause autism,
You'd probably have a world full of better people
Because I was kind, good, wise, fair, righteous, and just,
But the people I looked up to my whole life?
The world at large?
Yeah, you suck.

So instead of being treated well, I was used.
My mother created the blueprint for how to do it.
My pastors and teachers took up her mantle when she died,
And the world around me took full advantage
While their Golden Rule was three words long.
I handed over the reins, the keys
In the name of letting things go around
So they might someday come back…

Decades later, I realized something:
My mother had not received from me what she gave me.
She got out of this existence unscathed.
I was left holding a lifetime of pain and torment,
and nobody to pass it to but myself.

Karma, as they say,
Is a bitch.

5-3-24

Architecture can't give
you traum-

Robert

Originally posted online as a response to the following image:

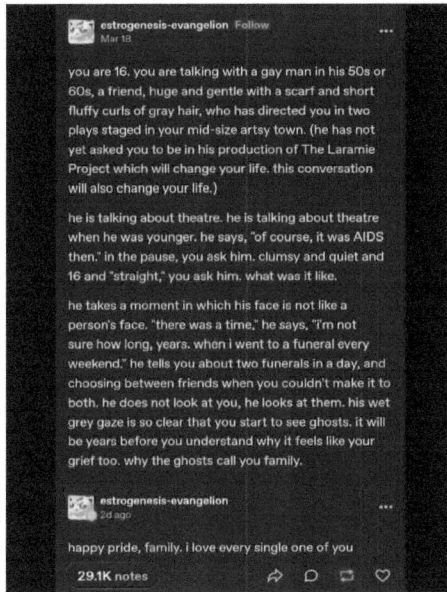

estrogenesis-evangelion Follow
Mar 18

you are 16. you are talking with a gay man in his 50s or 60s, a friend, huge and gentle with a scarf and short fluffy curls of gray hair, who has directed you in two plays staged in your mid-size artsy town. (he has not yet asked you to be in his production of The Laramie Project which will change your life. this conversation will also change your life.)

he is talking about theatre. he is talking about theatre when he was younger. he says, "of course, it was AIDS then." in the pause, you ask him. clumsy and quiet and 16 and "straight," you ask him. what was it like.

he takes a moment in which his face is not like a person's face. "there was a time," he says, "i'm not sure how long, years. when i went to a funeral every weekend." he tells you about two funerals in a day, and choosing between friends when you couldn't make it to both. he does not look at you, he looks at them. his wet grey gaze is so clear that you start to see ghosts. it will be years before you understand why it feels like your grief too. why the ghosts call you family.

estrogenesis-evangelion
2d ago

happy pride, family. i love every single one of you

29.1K notes

There was a summer camp I used to go to: CTY (Center for Talented Youth). Some of y'all, the OGs on my friends list are friends from then.

In 2002, I took a class called, "The Critical Essay: Popular Culture." This was at the Carlisle, PA location, session II at Dickinson College. Our teacher's name was Robert. I don't remember his last name. It was basically a media literacy class—something more people need to take. I was 14.

I don't remember a single one of my other teachers' names from CTY, but I remember Robert. He was gay and out, and he was one of the first openly gay people I knew. He had us watch *Little Shop of Horrors* and *West Side Story*, which I was familiar with, and *Hairspray*, which I was not, as well as various other media. He opened my eyes in so many ways.

One day, when we came back from lunch, the subject of the AIDS epidemic came up. To a group of 14- and 15-year-old girls in 2002, it was already pretty ancient history. But then Robert spoke. He told us about seeing all his friends slowly die of a mysterious illness. How it wasn't addressed by authorities. How they were shunned and cast away. How an entire population vanished in just a few years.

He told us about his boyfriend becoming ill and dying.

He spoke for only a few minutes, but we were rapt. You could have heard a pin drop. He brought those men alive again. We were horrified at what he experienced, and I felt it personally, though at the time, I didn't understand why.

It took me a long time to understand why.

I have no idea where Robert is, 22 years later, or if he is even still alive. But my life turned on those few minutes. He taught me more in a three-week course than many people have taught me in the span of years. I hope wherever he is, he has some idea that he made a difference in my life. He helped me, at least, if no one else. I am sure he helped others, but his legacy, and the legacy of those men, made it to me.

I am so grateful, every Pride, and the rest of the year, for their sacrifice, that I can live the life I do, and I hope to continue making my own sacrifices so that the next generations will have it better still. That is how we grow strong. That is how we endure.

6-7-24

Advice

"Smile.
Don't cry—I'll give you something to cry about.
Don't make that face.
Don't pout—your face will get stuck that way."

Be happy.
Swallow every sad feeling.
Don't show my tears, my pain.
Don't be an inconvenience.
Be grateful, always grateful—
Always smiling, always cheerful.

You were right about one thing, Mommy:
After 36 years,
My face did get stuck this way...

8-21-24

To Tanya, So We Can Both Stop Being Sad

I heard a song today and thought of you.
Though, I must confess
That happens fairly often…
I tend to put songs
I hear you listen to on my playlists.
Then, months or years later,
I'm reminded of the time I heard you listening,
Even if you've moved on from that song;
Like an audible snapshot of your taste in music.

You used to do silly dances as your songs played,
And sometimes, I imagine you're there with me,
Listening and doing a silly dance.

I'm often alone
And lonely,
But as long as I still have your songs
And those fabricated dance moves,
We're never really apart.

Love,
    MCishka

8-24-24

Our lives are
made up of a vast
collection of souls,
living and dead, and if
we are lucky, we pass
them along.

Therapy Worksheet: I Am

I am MC.
I wonder why and how and where and who.
I hear a thousand voices lifted up in song.
I see the problems in the world around me.
I want to be a change.
I am MC.

I pretend everything is okay even when it isn't.
I feel alone even when I am standing in a crowd.
I touch the lives of everyone around me but
I worry I will be forgotten.
I cry out at every injustice that I see.
I am MC.

I understand that I understand very little.
I say words that often go unheard.
I dream of a brighter future.
I try my best at all times and
I hope that others do too.
I am MC.

2-21-25

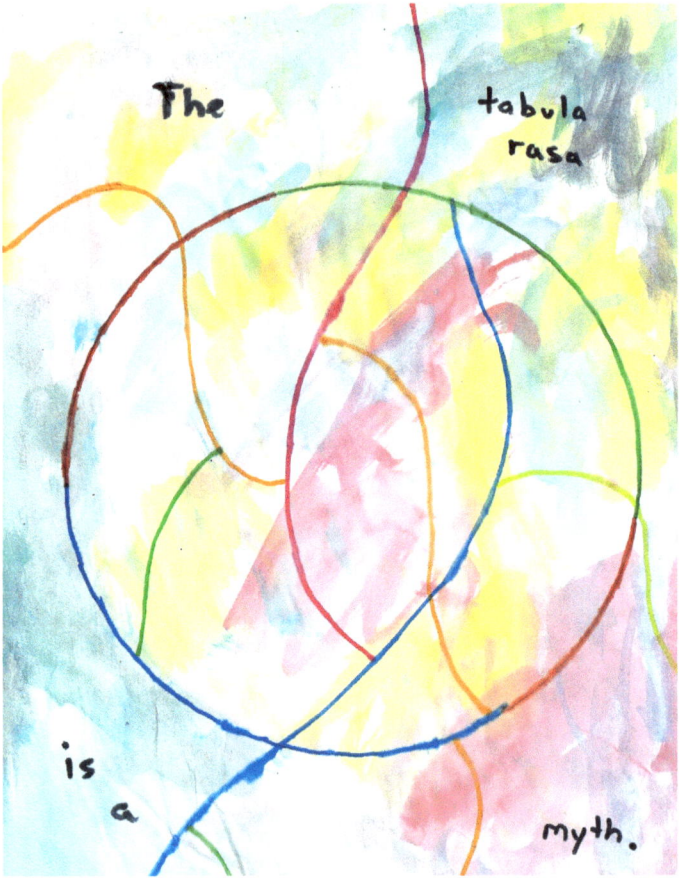

The tabula rasa is a myth.

Good Ol' #3

Once upon a time,
Billions of years ago,
A long time ago in a galaxy far, far away,
In the beginning,
A star exploded with *passion,*
Creating some fancy space dust
So that here, now
On Earth,
In North America,
On the Allegheny Plateau,
In the mid-Ohio Valley,
In February 2025,
I am constantly thirsty
And always have to piss.

2-22-25

This Is My Brain.

The universe is a soap bubble. Pop!
It has both popped and never popped.
Schröedinger's universe. Schröedinger's soap bubble.
This is why I don't like to do the dishes.

No stable ground to build a future.
A house built upon the sand will wash away.

Now you see me, now you don't.
Again and again and again and again and again.
Yeah, Yeah, Yeah, Yeah, Yeah…

You know how like the floor is lava?
The air is peacock feathers

It's always darkest before the dawn.
Dawn of A New Day.
You've met with a terrible fate, haven't you?

Entropy: the wind up, wind down.
It's pitch black, foul ball.
Black hole event horizon: always the bridesmaid, never the bride.
Now for the main event: popcorn, applejacks, criss-cross applesauce.
Tell your teacher to get lost!

Skeletons in the closet.
Come out of the closet, George.
OMG, they were roommates! Historical besties.

Alone in the dark. A portrait in the attic.
Writing novels in the castle
b/c you don't want to fuck Lord Byron *again*.

Frankenstein was also the monster.
Monsters are real: they live inside us.
I am the monster under my bed.
I am the monster inside of my head.

Nothing comes from nothing—nothing ever could.
Tabula rasa is a lie. The cake is a lie.
Carrot cake. Does anyone carrot all?
Hallelujah! He is risen indeed.

This is my brain, properly medicated:

    simply one thought
    after another
    after another
    after another.

No delusions.
    No time loops,
    no simulations,
    and thankfully,
    I am not God

No paranoia.
    Nobody hates me.
    I'm not unbearably annoying.
    Nobody is conspiring to get me.

No hallucinations.
    I do miss the background music
    and the occasional smell of baking bread
    for no reason.

Just me—
    able to think,
    able to plan,
    able to do.

    able to have relationships,
    able to connect with my friends.

    able to grieve a life lost
    for so long to this illness but also
    able move past it

Hello, Reader! My name is MC, and this is my brain on autism, PTSD, and schizoaffective disorder. I'm so glad that I finally know myself because I can begin to live my life.

How are you?

6/25 – 7/25

Acknowledgements

Thank you to the doctors, nurses, therapists, and techs at Hickory Behavioral Health Center in Cambridge, OH and at the Behavioral Health Unit at Camden Clark Medical Center in Parkersburg, WV, for providing a supportive environment in which to create much of this book's contents. Without you, the material within would be significantly poorer.

Also thanks to the patients at both hospitals, whose stays overlapped mine and who saw this content first, in its raw form, and indulged my preening and peacocking. Thank you for your friendship and validation. Sometimes we just need to hear we're good at something, especially in the darkness.

Thank you to my amazing support network of friends, colleagues, and therapists who weighed in with valuable insight. I trust in your wisdom, especially at times when my vision is clouded.

Thank you especially to the staff at A Mission For Michael's Rose House in Annandale, VA, who helped me get much needed answers, especially Tamika, Brooklyn, Naz, Jazz, Nuesha, Aja, Z, and last, but not least, Judith. And thank you to the patients at Rose House as well. You guys are honestly some of the coolest friends I've ever made.

Thank you to Tumblr user estrogenesis-evangelion for allowing me to use a screenshot of your post in this book. Super cool of you!

To my editors, Vanessa and Eva, thank you so much for your help in preparing this manuscript. I never would have gotten this far without you!

Thanks most especially to my best friends, Mike, Ashlee, and Tanya. You have stood beside me unflinchingly through both good times and bad. May we walk many more roads together. Love you to the moon and back!

Image credit Aja Somerville

About the Author

MC Augstkalns has a Masters in Linguistics from Ohio University. They live in Vienna, WV, with their six cats, two axolotls, and numerous fish. In addition to livestreaming on Twitch, they steward a Little Free Library to pass the time. One day, they hope to start a non-profit for LGBTQ+ individuals, women, and children in their hometown… when they aren't writing fanfiction. You can find them online at mcaugstkalns.com.

www.ingramcontent.com/pod-product-compliance
Lightning Source LLC
LaVergne TN
LVHW010031070426
835508LV00005B/294